An interview with

Michelle
Magorian

by Kate Agnew

mammoth

Other authors in the *Telling Tales* series:
Theresa Breslin, Gillian Cross, Anne Fine
Michael Morpurgo, Jenny Nimmo

Kate Agnew has worked as a children's bookseller
since reading English at St Anne's College, Oxford, and
currently manages Heffers Children's Bookshop in
Cambridge. She has written reviews for *The Guardian*
and *TES*, and articles for various children's book
magazines. She is a contributer to the forthcoming
Cambridge Guide to Children's Literature and has won
a special award for her contribution to
the National Year of Reading.

Published in Great Britain 1999 by Mammoth, an imprint of Egmont Children's
Books Limited, 239 Kensington High Street, London W8 6SA.

Interview questions, design and typesetting © 1999 Egmont Children's Books
Interview answers © 1999 Michelle Magorian
Michelle's Books © 1999 Kate Agnew

ISBN 0 7497 3863 4

A CIP catalogue record for this title is available from the British Library.

Printed and bound in Great Britain
by Cox & Wyman Ltd, Reading, Berks.

Contents

An interview with Michelle Magorian

by Kate Agnew

Michelle's Books

Michelle Magorian (b.1948) worked in theatre, television and film, before becoming a highly-acclaimed children's author. Her first book, *Goodnight Mister Tom*, won many awards, including the Guardian Children's Fiction Award, and was made into an award-winning film for television. Other titles include *Back Home* (winner of the American Library Association Award and the West Australian Young Readers Book Award), *A Little Love Song*, *Cuckoo in the Nest* and *A Spoonful of Jam*.

Michelle Magorian
by Kate Agnew

My childhood home

Where were you born?

Southsea, Hampshire.

What was the nearest town and what did you like best about it?

Portsmouth. In my late teens I used any excuse to go into the King's Theatre there. It was a large Victorian theatre; Henry Irving and Ellen Terry performed in it. I even sneaked into the auditorium and sat in the dark watching a new company set up. They had pre-London shows. I saw Neil Simon's *Barefoot in the Park* with Daniel Massey and *The Prime of Miss Jean Brodie* starring Vanessa Redgrave.

Although painfully shy, it was a wonderful refuge for me. It's still there.

Who did you get on with best?

I got on with both my brothers. I was both very bossy towards and very protective of them.

Were any animals part of the household?

My brother Jeremy once had a pet bantam, but it kept waking the neighbours at 5am so we drove out to a farm and left it there. Then he had an aviary but a cat got into it. He was so devastated he wanted to have the dead birds stuffed.

We had the odd visiting cat, which we had to shoo off as my mother was terrified of them!

In Singapore, where I lived from the age of three months to three, I had a dog called Chunky, who used to sleep under my cot, but I can't remember him.

My family

What did your family consist of?

Mother, Father, two brothers, Jeremy and Simon, born

when I was five and ten years old. (And, briefly, Lee Kim who looked after me when I was a baby and toddler.)

Michelle (left), Jeremy and their cousins in Ireland.

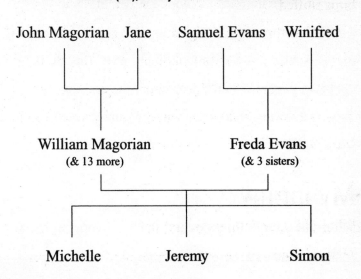

John Magorian   Jane   Samuel Evans   Winifred

William Magorian   Freda Evans
(& 13 more)   (& 3 sisters)

Michelle   Jeremy   Simon

Did your grandparents play any part in your family?

My Irish grandmother died of TB after giving birth to her ninth child in 14 years. My father was the eldest – he was 14. My grandfather then had five more children by a second wife. Aged 10–18 I saw my Irish grandfather for two weeks a year and I have lovely memories of him.

My Welsh grandfather died when I was a baby. I have 'inherited' some of his traits: an unconventional clergyman, he loved Shakespeare, Dickens and Tolstoy and worked on his sermons by pacing up and down. We saw my granny on Sundays. She used to give wonderful high teas with Welsh cakes, ginger and chocolate cake. She had long white hair with a blonde streak in it and collected rainwater in a bucket to wash it in. She used to wear it in a bun. It was fascinating to watch her do it. She had a place for everything and everything in its place, but the order made a refreshing break from the chaos of home.

Was your childhood happy?

I had some wonderful times and some unhappy nightmarish times. Aged 10–18 was the worst.

What is your best memory of it?

Camping with the scouts – lying awake at night, sleeping in a tent when it rained, singing round a campfire; making people laugh on stage; the annual dance show; rehearsals when I should have been having lessons.

What made you happy?

Camping, performing, dancing, reading, rehearsing, standing in the wings, singing, trampolines, walking, going to the theatre and cinema, being with my friends.

What is your worst memory of it?

Hiding in my bedroom when I was ten years old and looking after my brother who was five as we listened to the shouting and crashing downstairs. Then my father calling me out and him standing at the foot of the stairs telling me my pregnant mother was going to stay with my granny and demanding who I was going to go with, her or him. And when I was too stunned, numb and in pain to answer he yelled at my brother and told him that everything his grandfather had told him was a lie and that there was no such thing as fairies, or Father

Michelle's parents.

Christmas. And I remember taking my sobbing brother
back into the bedroom and holding him, deciding I
wouldn't have either of them and that I would look after
Jeremy and keep the family together that way. I became
middle-aged in seconds; I caught up with my childhood
later though!

What made you sad?

The last day of the summer term, knowing I had two
months at home to get through.

What were your first words?

My first words were, 'The boys were very rough, weren't they', aged three years, when my father was tucking me up in bed. I hadn't said one word before then and my parents had been worrying.

My schooldays

What was your first school like?

Very caring, it was the junior part of a convent. I went to two schools in Australia. (We lived there from when I was seven to when I was nine-and-a-half.) I had nightmares at the first and was moved to Kilbreda College in Mentone where I did very well but was a little naughty.

Who was your favourite teacher?

My dance teachers and elocution teacher, and a young visiting teacher who brought history alive.

Who was your most hated teacher?

I didn't have one.

When did you learn to read? Was it hard?

I can't remember, but I won a reading prize when I was five. I picked it up very quickly.

What was your secondary school like?

Wonderful; a convent school in the country with nuns who loved us and nurtured our individual talents.

What was your favourite subject?

Drama and English.

What was your most hated subject?

Geography.

Who was your favourite teacher there?

Mrs Kent; in Form 1 she called me her dormouse because I seemed to wake up in the summer term.

What was your best subject?

English.

What was your worst subject?

Geography.

What was your handwriting like then?

Like now; swings from indecipherable to neat.

Did any teacher think you might become a writer?

I think Miss Quinn – my geography teacher!

What are your first memories of reading?

Being frightened by my reading prize, *The Tale Of Samuel Whiskers*. I remember breaking out into a sweat the first time I read it to my elder son.

What did reading mean to you?

Escape and, later, discovery.

What did words mean to you?

Access to a world outside my own and insights into areas where I was confused.

This way, and that, she peers, and sees.
silver fruit upon silver trees; ✓

21st May. 1958.

Composition.

One day as the twins were walking across
the park they noticed a very old house. It
looked weird and spooky. The twins who
loved adventure decided to explore it that
night. When they went to bed Simon one
of the twins put an alarm clock under his
pillow and set the alarm for 12 o, clock. It
was 1 minute to 12 now, the alarm went
off. Simon scrambled out of bed and was

Michelle's handwriting.

10

Were you shy or talkative, solitary or sociable?

All four, still am!

Who was your favourite children's author?

Enid Blyton, Arthur Ransome.

When did you start reading adult authors?

Aged about 16; plays by Terrence Rattigan, the poems of Wilfred Owen and I loved Neil Simon. The war poets had a tremendous effect on me. When I was a student someone introduced me to Tolstoy and I went head over heels. I remember walking on my own in Paris in the snow and imagining I was in Russia. I also loved plays. I read *Barefoot in the Park* by Neil Simon in the library and had to leave I was laughing so much. When I went to college I had a craze for American playwrights, Arthur Miller, Tennessee Williams. I would save up my grant money so that I could go and see a matinée.

Did you read poetry?

Yes, World War I poets and, later, the Liverpool poets.

Did you read non-fiction?

Yes, psychology and Stanislavski.

What was your favourite non-fiction book?

Tricky! In my teens, *An Actor Prepares* or *Preparing A Character* by Stanislavski, and a tiny 30s book on introducing psychology including full explanations of introversion, extroversion, regression, etc.

What sport did you like?

Trampolining.

What sport do you enjoy now?

Swimming, going to the gym (if I get the chance!)

What music did you listen to?

Musicals, popular classics, the Beatles and pop music.

Was music important to you then?

Yes.

Is it now?

Yes.

What music do you listen to now?

Stephen Sondheim's and other musicals, some classical.

Did you enjoy painting?

Yes, but hardly did any at all.

Do you enjoy painting now, or looking at paintings?

I like looking at paintings. I really admire the ability
to draw.

**What part did cinema, drama and television play in
your life then?**

A lot.

What part do they play now?

I don't have much time as a single mother; I haven't
been to the cinema in years, but I've started going to the
theatre again.

Who was your favourite film or TV star then?

Jerry Lewis – he made me laugh when I was 8 or 9.

Who is your favourite now?

Judi Dench.

What is your favourite film?

I Know Where I'm Going, a 1940s black and white film with a very young Wendy Hillier.

My Career

What did you do when you left school?

My further education was at: The Rose Bruford College of Speech and Drama, 1966–1969 and at L'école Internationale de Mime, Marcel Marceau in Paris, 1969–1970.

What was your first job?

Rumplestiltskin for the Argyl Theatre for Youth.

Why did you decide to do it?

It was touring (I had itchy feet), it was my first Equity contract (difficult to get), and it was a big part.

Michelle in *Patches*, her mime show.

How long did you stay in it?

For the autumn.

What did you do next and why?

There was a job waiting for me at the Q20 Theatre
Company in Yorkshire. It was a wonderful opportunity
not only to act, but to write dialogue and songs, to sing

Michelle (left) in *Rookery Nook* at Perth Theatre.

Michelle preparing for her role as the Monkey Wife.

and to leap around. There were lots of wonderful talented people in the company and we did everything – sewing, painting – a huge variety of work.

After my contract finished in the summer I was offered a year's work with the Orchard Theatre Company in Devon. Again, it was a chance to do an enormous variety of roles in a touring company which lived and worked together in a very committed and caring way.

I then stopped touring. I suddenly wanted to stay put. I was offered a job at a repertory company where I only had to act! I continued working in repertory theatre in Perth, Newcastle, Leeds, Birmingham, Worcester, Northampton, Basingstoke, Watford Palace Theatre, Windsor Palace

Theatre, Shaftesbury Theatre, the Young Vic,
Colchester. I did half musicals and half plays, acting
'character' parts and leaning towards comedy.

I also did my quota of hairy creatures, Orinoco
Womble, Paddington Bear and the Monkey Wife in the
musical of that name.

My career as a writer

Did you write as a child?

Yes – stories. While I was training to become an actress I
wrote masses of very sad poetry, and some funny poems
for special occasions like people's birthdays.

When did you decide to become a professional writer?

In my 30s, I joined a novel-writing class and the tutor
Dulan Barber, who was also a writer, persuaded me to
send my manuscript of *Goodnight Mister Tom* to the
agent Pat White, who loved it and sent it to a publisher.

How and when did you start to write?

In 1970, scripts and lyrics in Q20. I carried on writing

odd lyrics and poetry and I kept journals and dream diaries, and wrote short stories and a novella. I also wrote a couple of plays at college.

Where did you get your idea for your first novel?

Goodnight Mister Tom began as one of a set of ten stories about colours, based on a song from *Joseph and the Amazing Technicolour Dreamcoat*. I was sitting in the launderette thinking about the colours green and brown, and I began to think of leaves and trees. Brown made me think of earthiness and stability and green made me think of youth and vulnerability. I thought of a young beech tree with a slim trunk and suddenly I saw a picture in my head of a small thin, frightened boy standing in a graveyard. I knew he was an evacuee because he had a label. He became William Beech.

My mother had been a nurse during the War. I remembered her telling me two stories, one about a boy who curled up under the hospital bed; he had never slept in a bed before. The other was about a boy whose underwear had been sewn together. His mother was furious when she realised that my mother had unpicked all the stitches.

Michelle's mother in her Q.A. uniform.

The tenth story in the collection was about the paint box that Tom Oakley had hidden in his cupboard. I wrote about Tom and his young wife Rachel and their idyllic days together. I couldn't get William Beech and Tom Oakley out of my head, I wanted to know what happened to them next. I spent years working on it and I couldn't contain my excitement when it was finished, but even then I had no intention of sending it to a publisher until I read a chapter of it aloud at my novel-writing class and the tutor persuaded me to send it off.

Where did your next novels come from?

Once I started researching for *Goodnight Mister Tom* there were so many more questions I wanted to ask. I came across a photograph of a group of English children on a liner returning to England after living in America for five years. I remembered the problem I had had returning to England after just two and a half years in Australia. And these children had been separated from their parents. The photograph wouldn't go away and eventually it became the beginning of *Back Home*.

I was born after the terrible winter of 1947 and I suppose I wanted to go back and find out more about the period. There is a theory that some people like writing about the time just before they were born. The period chose me really.

I'm interested in the theatre in the 1940s; people who were working then are still alive and I wanted to bring it back to life. I met a director who had started by doing odd jobs for the theatre. He'd been evacuated for five years and wanted to stay in the country.
He wanted to be a farmer but his father insisted on bringing him back. He started doing an apprenticeship and in the evenings he did work for the local variety theatre. It got into his blood and he was hooked. He ended up being head of drama at a university. That was the seed of *Cuckoo in the Nest*.

When I came to *A Spoonful of Jam* I wanted to develop the characters more. I wanted to know more about the incident where Elsie had to be rescued, and I came across an interview with a grammar school girl who went hop-picking. She had to leave early to go back to school, unlike her cousins, and she didn't really feel part of either life. I was fascinated too by the cold winter of 1947 and the hot summer that came after it, when I was born. I researched the weather; one time I went into a newspaper library and just looked at weather forecasts. It was a mosaic really; I started to daydream little bits here and little bits there.

Who encouraged or dissuaded you?

My mother liked to hear my stories. My teachers, however, were not so keen. One teacher used to tell me off for writing stories.

What, if any, writer influenced you?

I don't know if he influenced me, but I admired him – Tolstoy. Even when a minor character appears only on one page he seems able to make them a fully rounded person and so vivid. One can see them scratching their nose and leaning against a mantelpiece. But I love Neil Simon too, and Ayckbourn and Michael Frayn. I love Michael Frayn's stuff; he's funny and intellectual as well.

Do you like being a writer?

Yes.

What do you like best about writing?

Writing dialogue.

Can you help being a writer?

No.

Is it an obsession or compulsion?

Compulsion.

Is it a lonely profession?

No, because you have the company of your fictional people and you meet people when carrying out research.

Do you find writing hard?

I have excruciatingly difficult days, and days when

I can't write fast enough for my thoughts.

Did you start with habits that you've since changed?
Can't think of any.

How long does it take to write a book?
If I'm not doing anything else, two years. *Goodnight Mister Tom* took me four years – three years to write the first draft, a year to re-write it. During the first three years I was writing it I was also working in repertory theatre which involves working six days and six nights a week, rehearsing one play during the day, performing another at night. I wrote on Sundays and in-between acting jobs. *A Little Love Song* took six to seven years from start to finish, but for two or three years of that time it was in the loft.

Do you have any rituals that you do before writing?
Scribbling a few notes.

Is there a pattern to the writing day?
Not since having children.

'No' he had said simply. 'He was a ~~boy~~ asc boy. I wonder ~~or~~ seventeen? Eighty years ago now. ~~And Elsie noticed Joan look up~~ ~~and the rising by picking her head down again~~. 'Schoolboy. Soldier. Labourer. A life so far,' he concluded.

On ~~Easter~~ ~~that~~ Good Friday ~~and Elsie~~ ~~~~ to a Whitbread Farm she had heard the group of actors and actresses would be performing Twelfth Night.

It was ~~~~ where Church Services + the Mayor set up the glass and watched the actors daft about, way their arms and spouty were!

'I don't understand a bleedin' word of this!' she heard a woman mutter to her. ~~and Elsie~~ ~~but didn't~~ ~~it didn't~~ ~~either~~ ~~it didn't~~ ~~~~ moment ~~~~ Malvolia ~~~~ plays a underful Jane ~~~~ making him believe ~~~~ on love with him ~~~~ what she was lying about the yellow stockings and cross gartering ~~~~ his legs. ~~olive~~ ~~the actors~~ posing ~~~~ and ~~~~ hovered on the stage amorous ~~~~ about and ~~~~ the ~~~~ on stage ~~~~ more ~~~~ Elsie's ~~~~ magic had brushed her ~~~~ unseen, so it was last she th

2440

Do you rewrite?

Lots.

When your story is finished, who reads your manuscript first?

I used to read it aloud to my ex-husband. Also I hand it over to a young person in case some of my research background is too obscure.

Do you listen to criticism?

Yes. I also disagree with it sometimes.

Why do you write for children?

I'm not sure why I write for children. Maybe I like looking at life through a young person's eyes. Perhaps I want to articulate what they're feeling. I'm not sure.

Where do your ideas come from?

Ideas come from photos, questions I want answered, overheard snippets of conversation, daydreams.

An example of Michelle's redrafting.

What subjects appeal to you?

Relationships between people and how they affect one
another.

What kind of research do you do?

Reading, interviews, newspapers, films.

How important is imagination?

Vital.

Do you base your situations on real life?

Not consciously.

Do you base your characters on real people?

No, but real people have sometimes snuck in.

What matters most – the story or the characters?

The characters. Their relationships with one another
create the story.

Who do you write for?

Me.

Which of your books is your favourite?

I don't have one.

Which is your favourite character in your own books?

Zach, Charlie, Elsie, Jessica, Rose, Miss Hilda, Dot –
I have many favourites.

Are pictures important in your books?

I write mostly for older children who I hope can create
pictures from my words.

What gives you most satisfaction about being a writer?

I love getting lost in another situation and having the
dialogue between the characters taking off, almost out
of my control, and being surprised with what they come
out with.

What do you dislike most about writing?

Sitting.

What do you hope to achieve with your books?

I want to connect readers with different kinds of people; I want readers to enjoy and care about the people I've invented, to be carried away by the story, to be watching a film in their heads.

Why is fiction important?

Fiction is important because it expands people's boundaries. It makes people feel less isolated when they can connect with the people they're reading about.

Will it still be important in the new century?

Of course.

Do you think TV can complement reading or be a substitute for it?

Complement.

Which book, either children's or adult, has influenced your life?

So many books have influenced my life; Tolstoy's *Anna*

Karenina, Six Bad Boys by Enid Blyton and Arthur Ransome's *Swallows and Amazons*.

Which book comforts you most?

At the moment *Life and How to Survive It* by John Cleese and Robin Skinner.

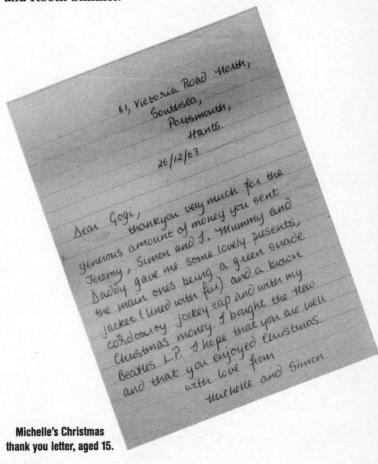

61, Victoria Road North,
Southsea,
Portsmouth,
Hants.

26/12/63

Dear Gogi,
thankyou very much for the generous amount of money you sent Jeremy, Simon and I. Mummy and Daddy gave me some lovely presents, the main ones being a green suede jacket (lined with fur) and a brown corderoy jockey cap and with my Christmas money I bought the new Beatles L.P. I hope that you are well and that you enjoyed Christmas.
with love from
Michelle and Simon.

Michelle's Christmas thank you letter, aged 15.

Cover artwork by Jessica Meserve for *A Little Love Song*

Michelle's Books
An overview by Kate Agnew

WHEN *Goodnight Mister Tom* was published in 1981 it met with immediate and widespread critical acclaim from adults and children alike, and Michelle Magorian was quickly established as a leading contemporary children's writer. Winner of the Guardian Children's Fiction Award and now regularly appearing on school reading lists, *Goodnight Mister Tom* remains enormously popular and is published in 10 different languages. The story of an abused child who escapes his brutal home life when he is evacuated to the countryside during World War II, it displays all the characteristics for which Michelle's work is now well-known and

Goodnight Mister Tom

loved. William Beech is unloved, uncared for and uneducated when he arrives in Little Weirwold, while Mister Tom, to whose home he is sent because his mother has insisted that he must be in sight of a church, appears a surly old man, made bitter by the untimely death of his wife and child many years before. The story that unfolds is one of love, friendship, patience and hard work.

Further novels

Since 1981 Michelle has published a further four novels, two picture books, two volumes of poetry and a number of short stories. The novels, for which she is best known, form part of a long tradition of writing for children in which family love, personal integrity and strong moral values are seen as central to the development of the main characters. The 'family' may not be the traditional family unit for William Beech any more than it is for Anne of Green

Gables, but for both the need for stability and a happy home is paramount.

Michelle's characters come to understand that it is not material things that create happiness. In *Cuckoo in the Nest* and *A Spoonful of Jam*, Ralph and Elsie Hollis, living in a cramped and overcrowded house are upset by their poverty only because it marks them out as different from their grammar school contemporaries. What really upsets them is their father's refusal to acknowledge the things that matter to them. In *Back Home*, Rusty initially misses her comfortable American lifestyle but comes to realise that it is not the physical comforts of smart clothes or central heating for which she longs, but the pleasure of being part of a large and loving family.

Cuckoo in the Nest

A Spoonful of Jam

Back Home

Believe in yourself . . .

In *Back Home*, as Rusty faces life with an unfamiliar family in a strange land, her adopted family offers her a set of rules by which to live her life: 'Believe in yourself,' they tell her, 'believe in others, and work like hell.' These instructions provide a set of values for all Michelle's characters as they confront the complex and changing world of Britain in the 1940s.

Self-belief does not come easily to the heroes and heroines of Michelle's novels. Even

Cuckoo in the Nest

characters like Ralph Hollis or Rusty, who appear initially to be brimming with self-confi-

Back Home

dence, have to go through a difficult period of change before they can begin to be sure of their own position. Self-confidence can only be secured within a loving home and each has to resolve their family problems before they can be certain of themselves.

At the beginning of *Back Home* Rusty is a happy and chatty girl, sure of her own opinions and secure in the love of her adopted American family. Dressed in her American teenagers' clothes she arrives back in Britain nervous but confident, asking her mother questions and talking about art and the theatre. Her confidence unnerves her mother who last encountered 'Rusty' – or Virginia as she prefers to call her – as a quiet, spindly-legged small child. Similarly Ralph's father cannot understand the differences in his son since he left home and went to live in a Cornish vicarage. For both Rusty and Ralph their parents' absence during their childhood and subsequent lack of understanding deals a severe blow to their self-confidence.

Cuckoo in the Nest

Parent trouble

The irony for both Ralph and Rusty is that their differences with their parents stem in part from their similarities. Mr Hollis acknowledges Ralph's inherited stubbornness with a degree of pride, while Rusty's mother finally joins Rusty in a truly independent life.

Both Rusty's father and Mr Hollis have been absent for a long time. Their return to family life is made especially difficult as they have just spent several years largely in the company of men. Mr Hollis loathes Ralph's 'Nancy boy' interest in the theatre, and neither father knows how to respond to his young daughter. Elsie recognises this and blames her sex. She is certain that her father would take pride in her and invite her to join him and Harry at the allotment – an invitation for which she longs – if only she was a boy. Finally she resorts to cutting her hair and dressing as a boy, but her father still doesn't seem to understand her.

World War II

All Michelle's novels are set during World War II and its aftermath. The period provides a powerful vehicle for the exploration of the changing nature of human relationships and the importance of family love and lasting friendship. Fathers have been absent from family life and women have learned new skills and independence, while children have grown up more quickly than their parents realise, straining the limits of family tolerance. Although the loving family is seen as the base from which each character can establish his or her own identity, the war has driven families apart. In each of the novels there is a marked tension between the image of happy family life for which the characters strive and the reality that confronts the young heroes and heroines as they struggle to establish their own identity, while those around them piece together their lives against a backdrop of war, poverty and hardship.

In Michelle's work the war allows a degree of independence that would never before have been possible, particularly for young women; for Rusty it means evacuation to America where *Back Home* the term 'teenager' has just been coined, and to a family free from the conventions of British society. For Rose and Diana in *A Little Love* *A Little* *Song* it brings a chance to plan their own lives *Love Song* away from the conventions that would otherwise restrict them. Rose, especially, gains the intellectual freedom to develop her writing and plan a future career.

For William Beech the war offers an opportunity to escape from the cruelty of his home life and to begin afresh with Mister Tom. None of Michelle's characters is more lacking in self-belief than William when he first arrives, sewn into his underwear for the winter and covered in bruises. But William flourishes under Mister Tom's tender care to become an integral part of his life, filling the gap that was left when his own child died. The link between love and self-confidence is made even more obvious when William returns to London and to his mother. The cruelty he experiences at his mother's hands is both shocking and disturbing. When the book was adapted for television in 1998 it was shown as an adult film, after the 9 o'clock watershed.

Independent women

One senses that, whenever the novels had been set, Michelle's heroines would have been strong independent women, but for all her women, young and old alike, the war brings the possibility of escape from routine domestic duties and a chance to demonstrate their skill outside the home. Rusty's mother has not only learned to drive and to fix cars, but has also found the independence necessary to leave her restrictive life and her old-fashioned husband, abandoning the values of her mother-in-law and setting up her own home. Rusty, like her mother, has to learn that life has changed for every generation and that her mother, too, deserves her independence.

Back Home

However, the lifestyle of women who choose to stay at home and care for their families is shown to be as important as that of their colleagues who go out to work. Ralph and Elsie's Aunty Win has clearly flourished during her

Cuckoo in the Nest

time in the WAAF and feels oppressed and undervalued when she returns home. She tries to encourage Ralph's mother to leave her family and join up, but Ralph takes his mum to a play celebrating the lives of women who have stayed at home caring for their families. For the women as well as the men in Michelle's novels, it is freedom of choice and the independence this brings that matter as much as the choices they eventually make.

A loving relationship

The war, however, is shown to have changed society's view of women irrevocably. The greatest social change of all is seen in Dot (*A Little Love Song*). Pregnant but unmarried, Dot's story mirrors that of Hilda, a woman who was in the same situation more than twenty years earlier, during World War I. Each had been in love with the dead father of their unborn child, but for Hilda their physical relationship led her own

A Little Love Song

father to lock her away in a mental asylum, while for Dot life will be manageable if she can only afford a pretend wedding ring.

Unlike many children's novelists, Michelle sees sex as an integral part of a happy loving relationship, and not something which should be condemned outside marriage. It is not, however, a necessary part of any friendship between boy and girl. When Rusty returns from America she is used to talking to boys as equals, knows the facts of life and is quite happy to have a friendship with a boy that is entirely platonic. For Rusty, Lance can both replace the family from whom she is becoming increasingly detached, and represent the America of her dreams. Her mother, however, is clearly horrified when she speaks to a boy, while her school is shocked that she should even think of addressing a boy in public. The other girls believe that Rusty could have got herself pregnant merely by being with a boy in her pyjamas.

Back Home

Curiosity and even disgust about sex are

Cuckoo in the Nest

seen to be entirely natural. Ralph is appalled at the prospect of his parents sleeping together and is visibly embarrassed at his mother's pregnancy, but when Isla comes back from the Isle of Wight, where she has been snowed in with her new husband, Ralph is eager to discover whether she appears any

A Little Love Song

different. Rose avidly reads Dot's pregnancy book in order to become better informed, and her knowledge turns out to be essential when Dot goes into labour.

For the young heroes of Michelle's novels the boundaries between friendship and first love are often blurred. In *A Little Love Song* Rose initially views Alec as a good friend, someone far too old to be considered

Cuckoo in the Nest

romantically. For Ralph Hollis, Jessica Egerton-Smythe is first a good friend; being obsessed with Isla he does not think of Jessica as a girlfriend until he comes to realise how much he misses her in her absence. Even then he still seems to play the role of a son in the family. Mrs Egerton-Smythe and Jessica mother him together, giving him the clothes that once belonged to Jessica's dead brother and encouraging him to start his own theatre wardrobe. The shift from brotherly love to romantic feeling is so gradual that even Ralph himself has to seek clarification from Jessica, needing to know for sure how she feels about him.

For all the main characters friendship is as important as sex in a happy relationship; Alec and Rose, like Jessica and Ralph, are friends before they become lovers. For Rose sex without love is a nightmare. Its clinical quality reminds her of an operation, but with Alec whom she loves, the experience is quite different; rather than feeling like a sacrificial lamb she feels herself 'dissolving into a delicious whirlpool'.

A Little Love Song

The support of friends and family

Rose and Alec's physical happiness mirrors their intellectual partnership. Alec is interested in books, writes himself and understands Rose's ambition to be a writer. Rose's relationship with Derry is unsatisfactory not least because Derry has no interest in Rose's work or in her inner world. In marked contrast Alec not only encourages her to write, but is responsible for her first publication, developing her self-confidence and believing in what she can do. It is this intertwining of self-belief and others' belief in their abilities that gives all the characters their inner strength and conviction. All are on the verge of adulthood, struggling to establish their own independence while longing for the strength, comfort and certainty offered by family and friends.

In the absence of family affection it is often friends who provide moral support and comfort. For William, Mister Tom becomes a second father, and for Ralph and Elsie the theatre provides a second home and an extended family. Mrs Egerton-Smythe also plays a vital role in the development of Ralph's career in the theatre. Although nominally Ralph's employer she not only provides props for the plays, houses members of the cast and allows him time off work to act, but more importantly she provides the advice and encouragement that Ralph's family cannot.

Although Ralph, like Rusty in *Back Home*, feels initially let down by his family and better supported by his friends, both Ralph and Rusty still feel a strong need for their families to believe in them and accept them for what they are. They have to learn to compromise if they want to be accepted by both family and friends. Although Ralph's father will never be happy that his son has picked the stage for a career, his intense dislike of the theatre is softened when he discovers that Ralph's acting hero is an old army friend. He even ends up acting himself, despite his fear of what his friends might say. For Rusty, too, compromises must be made; her father will never understand her desire for freedom and her failure to conform, but eventually Rusty learns that her mother's approval and understanding are enough.

Back Home

Humour

The books deal with powerful emotions and difficult issues – family separations, wartime losses, abuse and neglect – yet all of Michelle's novels exhibit their author's irrepressible sense of humour. We cannot help but laugh at Aunty Win's ghoulish and enthusiastic response to news of murder or – even better – suicide in the newspaper, while Ralph's struggle to carry a stuffed life-sized bear down the busy streets of Winford is unforgettable.

Cuckoo in the Nest

Perhaps most memorable of all is the scene in *A Little Love Song* where Rose, out at her

A Little Love Song

first dance but suddenly determined to do her bit towards household economy, fills her capacious bloomers with left-over orange peel, bent on making marmalade. However, as she jitterbugs around the dance floor the elastic of her ancient, heavy black knickers finally gives way to shower her – and everyone around her – with orange peel. Rose is appalled but for the reader – as for the appreciative GIs – it is a moment of high comedy.

Theatre

Michelle's characters all share their author's love of acting and the theatre. Against the backdrop of the 1940s, the theatre represents a means of escape from the humdrum world of blackouts, rationing and wartime regulations. For both Ralph and Elsie the theatre offers a taste of the adult world, a chance to make new friends and to enter into a new lifestyle.

Cuckoo in the Nest

Although Ralph is initially an outsider in the world of the theatre, lacking either the money or the training to qualify him for the job he wants, he is quickly accepted and valued for the work he does, rapidly becoming part of the large and supportive theatre family who share in his passions and interests.

The theatre possesses almost magical qualities, liberating him from everyday worries and offering friendship, moral support and, eventually, paid work and a career. For Elsie it is even more magical, removing her from all her problems at one fell swoop with an undreamed of offer of a major part and a protector who helps her to overcome her shyness and fear of being bullied.

A Spoonful of Jam

Goodnight Mister Tom

Even William Beech demonstrates his growing self-confidence as he progresses from reluctant prompter to actor in his own right. William is able to overcome his shyness as he pretends to be a different person, but for Elsie

Hollis, used to acting a part both at school and at home, the joy of being in the theatre is that it allows her to be herself. On her return to school her experience in the theatre paves the way for her to be accepted by her contemporaries and her teachers.

Education

Ralph and Elsie gain access to the world of the theatre because of their education; their grammar school background allows them to cut across class divides – though it is this same education which leads to Elsie being bullied and Ralph being mistrusted by his father. For all the characters education is of vital importance, and is often seen as the first step towards allowing them to grow away from their social and family background.

William Beech appears to have received no education at all when he comes to Little Weirwold, and the teaching Mister Tom gives him is almost as important as the love and affection. For William learning to read means not just acquiring a new skill, but gaining the freedom to join his friends in his rightful classroom.

Back Home   For Rusty, too, education is equated with both happiness and independence. In America she was a bright and happy child who did well at school, but in Britain she is viewed as stupid since she knows nothing of British history, Latin or algebra, and speaks always in what her contemporaries regard as 'slang'. Michelle satirises the world of the girls' boarding school, which allows no space for individuality of expression and cares less for educating its girls than for producing 'young women who would make good wives and mothers'. Bereft of both education and family love, Rusty feels abandoned and isolated, living only for the time when she can escape to the derelict cottage and be herself.

Happiness at a price

Rusty eventually finds happiness when she returns to the country and moves to a school where pupils are encouraged to think and act independently. Rusty has to pay a price for independence, however; the house they love has become their own only because of the death of a beloved friend and, in choosing to live with her mother, Rusty incurs her father's extreme displeasure and his threat to 'cut them all off without a penny'. For all Michelle's heroes and heroines, happiness demands a high price. They not only have to work hard, but must be prepared to make sacrifices in order to achieve happiness eventually. For the reader, however, it is this very struggle that makes their eventual happiness so appealing. The world of Michelle's books is not that of a fairy-tale land where everyone can expect to live happily ever after, but a captivating and believable world in which hard work and determination, coupled with the desire to love and to be loved, can finally bring characters the happiness they deserve.

Kate Agnew
1999

Bibliography
In date order

Goodnight Mister Tom
Kestrel Books 1981

William Beech is evacuated to the country to live with Tom Oakley at the start of World War II. A lonely child, he finds care and comfort with the surly old man.

Winner of the Guardian Children's Fiction Award 1981, the International Reading Association Children's Book Award 1982 and the West Australian Young Readers Book Award; runner-up for the 1981 Young Observer Award; Shortlisted for the Carnegie Book Award.
BAFTA Award-winning TV film 1998

Back Home
Viking 1985

When Virginia ('Rusty') is sent back to live in England after being evacuated to America during the war, she finds Britain a poverty-stricken and depressing place where even her own family seem strangers. Gradually she learns to think of the strange country as home and begins to understand the way of life there.

*Winner of the American Library Association Best Book for Young
Adults 1984 and the West Australian Young Readers Book Award
TV Film 1989, screenplay by David Wood
Dramatised for BBC Radio 4*

Waiting For My Shorts To Dry

Viking, 1989, illustrated by Jean Baylis

A collection of poems for young children published in picture book format with colour illustrations.

Who's Going To Take Care Of Me?

Harper & Row, US 1990, illustrated by James Graham Hale

Orange Paw Marks

Viking 1991, illustrated by Jean Baylis

A collection of poems based on events children will recognise from their own experience.

A Little Love Song

Methuen 1991, Mammoth 1998

In 1943 17-year-old Rose and her older sister Diana are sent to a seemingly sleepy village to keep them out of

Michelle
Magorian

Author of *Goodnight Mister Tom*

A Little

Love

Song

harm's way. When their chaperone fails to turn up, the two girls experience their first taste of independence and Rose finds herself falling in love for the first time.

Jump
Walker 1992, illustrated by Jan Ormerod

A picture book about a boy who wants to dance although his mother wants him to play basketball.

In Deep Water
Viking 1992

A collection of short stories about water and the sea.

Cuckoo In The Nest
Methuen 1994

During World War II Ralph has been evacuated to a Cornish vicarage where he has acquired an accent and a way of life that his father cannot understand. Ralph wants to pursue a career in the theatre, but his father is equally convinced that the theatre is only for sissies. Ralph's father is horrified when Ralph loses his respectable job at the mill, but Ralph is determined to find work at the theatre.

A Spoonful Of Jam

Methuen 1998

Ralph's younger sister Elsie feels an outsider everywhere. At school her accent isn't posh enough, on the streets she is bullied for being a grammar school girl, and at home her father cannot understand her love of books and reading. It is only when she visits Ralph at the theatre that she discovers a way of resolving her difficulties.

Background: cover artwork by David Axtell for *A Spoonful of Jam*

Short Stories

'The Front Room' in *They Wait and Other Stories*

Pepper Press 1983

Compiled by Lance Salway, illustrated by Jill Bennett

'Beginners' in *Guardian Angels*

Viking Kestrel 1987

Compiled by Stephanie Nettell, illustrated by Mike Daley

'The Greatest' in *You're Late Dad*

Methuen Children's Books 1989

Edited by Tony Bradman

'The Smile' in *Love Them, Hate Them*

Methuen Children's Books 1991

Edited by Tony Bradman

'Whiting' in *Stage Struck*

Hamish Hamilton, 1991

Edited by Jean Richardson

Scripts
You and Me

BBC Schools television

Sea Change

with Stephen Keeling & Peter Venner, 1998